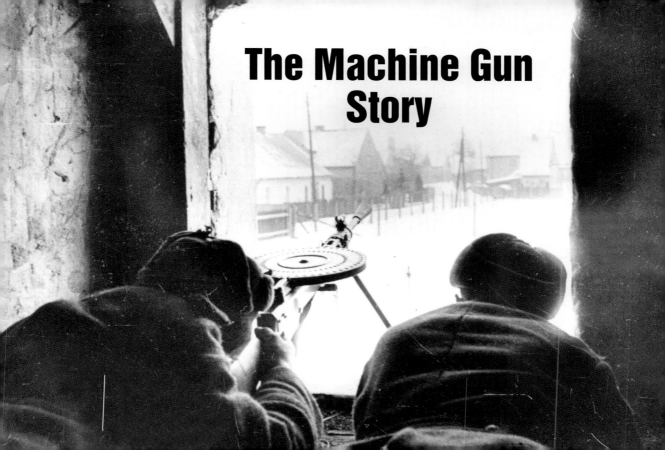

The Machine Gun Story

The Machine Gun Story

Chris McNab

The
History
Press

Also in this series:

The Concorde Story
The Spitfire Story
The Vulcan Story
The Red Arrows Story
The Harrier Story
The Dam Busters Story
The Hurricane Story
The Lifeboat Story
The Tornado Story
The Hercules Story

Published in the United Kingdom in 2010 by
The History Press
The Mill · Brimscombe Port · Stroud · Gloucestershire · GL5 2QG

British Library Cataloguing in Publication Data
A catalogue record for this book is available from the British
Library.

ISBN 978-0-7524-5234-0

Half title page: *The Degtyarev DPM was a Soviet
7.62mm LMG, an improved version of the earlier DP.
It fired from a 47-round flat pan magazine, and was
a popular weapon with ground troops.*
Half title page verso: *The Browning M2HB
soldiers on, here in its Quick-Change Barrel (QCB)
modification, which as its name suggests allows for
more rapid barrel changes.*

➤ *British troops fire the M1928 Thompson SMG.
Thompsons could be loaded with either 18-, 20- or
30-round box magazines, or 50- or 100-round drum
magazines.*

Typesetting and origination by The History Press
Printed in Italy by L.E.G.O. S.p.A.

CONTENTS

Acknowledgements   6
Introduction   7

Maxim's Gun   17
The First Gas Guns   33
World War I   45
Light and Aviation Machine Guns   56
American Giants and Inter-War Development 67
World War II   84
The Post-War World   99
Submachine guns   114
Epilogue   125

Glossary   126
Bibliography   128

ACKNOWLEDGEMENTS

I would like to thank Jo de Vries of The History Press for her editorial support in the development of this book, and for her valued friendship. Gratitude also goes to Ted Neville at Cody Images for supplying an excellent range of photographs for this title. Final thanks go to my wife and family, for enduring my writer's life.

All images in this book have been supplied courtesy of Cody Images:
http//www.codyimages.com

By the beginning of the 1880s, the flintlock, muzzle-loading era of firearms was drifting deeper into memory. The development of unitary cartridges – ammunition that contains case, powder, bullet and primer in one unit – had made breech-loading firearms (guns loaded from the rear, breech end rather than the muzzle) a possibility. For the general mass of soldiery, this eventually meant the adoption of the bolt-action rifle, first pioneered by Swiss gunsmith Johann Nikolaus von Dreyse in 1836, then perfected over subsequent decades via legendary names such as Peter Paul Mauser and Ferdinand von Mannlicher. The advantages of the bolt-action cartridge rifle when compared to the flintlock were profound. A typical infantryman in around 1800, wielding his smoothbore flintlock, would be lucky to fire off more than three rounds per minute, suffered regular misfires, and had an accurate range of roughly 150m (492ft). Jump forward 80 years and an infantryman armed with a magazine-fed bolt-action rifle could fire up to 15 rounds per minute, command lethal

▼ The MG42, by the time it was developed in the early years of World War II, represented 60 years of progress in machine gun technology and tactical applications.

7

➤ *The Vandenberg gun, a nineteenth-century battery fire weapon. Note the screw-thread breech block at the rear with cartridges already fixed in place ready for loading.*

Did you know?

During a demonstration *c*.1718, the Puckle gun managed to fire 63 shots in seven minutes, about three times more than a musket-armed infantryman could achieve.

ranges of more than 1,500 yards (1,371m) and had a gun that kept on working, largely regardless of weather conditions.

Yet for all the great advances in firearms technology, it remained the case that the rate at which an infantryman could fire was limited by the manual action of reloading – the physical process of operating the bolt backwards (to eject the spent cartridge case) and forwards (to load the new cartridge). Such is why other gunmakers set their minds to a new challenge, how to deliver what we know today as automatic fire.

There were some precedents. In 1718, British writer and inventor James Puckle produced a single-barrel 1in-calibre weapon that was fed by a nine-chamber hand-rotated magazine, both the magazine and the flintlock mechanism operated by a winding handle. This gun was actually more prescient than much of what followed over the next 150 years. Early attempts at providing a single gunner with heavy firepower tended to revolve around simply multiplying the number of barrels and actions used. ('Action' refers to the operating parts of the gun responsible for cartridge feed, cartridge ejection and firing.) The US Vandenberg gun of the mid-nineteenth century, for example, featured a total of between 85 and more than 100 rifled barrels in a brass screw breech, each barrel loaded separately and then fired simultaneously by turning a large winding handle at the rear of the drum. Needless to say, the Vandenberg gun was enormously impractical, the disadvantages of the extended reloading time far outweighing the advantage of a concentrated split-second burst. A more convincing possibility

Did you know?
The concept of repeating weapons goes back into the pre-Christian era. The Chinese, for example, were using a type of repeating crossbow in the third century BC.

came with the French-designed Montigny Mitrailleuse, which had a more reserved 25 barrels. These were fired individually rather than en masse, and speed reloading was possible via a 25-cartridge magazine block. The Mitrailleuse actually saw some combat during the 1870s, but it was generally misunderstood at a tactical level (it was treated as a small artillery piece), and its bulky set-up meant that its practicality was limited.

Then, in 1861, came the forerunner of the true machine gun. In that year the American inventor Dr Richard Jordan Gatling presented the Gatling gun. It was again a multi-barrelled (six, later 10 barrels) weapon powered manually by hand, but the arrangement was revolutionary (although with glances back towards the Puckle gun). The .45/70 cartridges were fed into the breech by a gravity-powered 'hopper' magazine set above the breech, and the barrels themselves rotated, via a hand-operated handle, around a central axis. Each barrel had its own firing mechanism. Turning the Gatling's operating handle rotated the barrels, each barrel picking up a cartridge as it passed the hopper and firing it at the bottom of the turn. The multi-barrel arrangement ensured that the individual barrels did not overheat (with respectful firing), and new stacks of ammunition could be dropped into the hopper even when the gun was in action.

The Gatling gun was a demonstrable success, and was used in combat not only in US and Central American conflicts from 1861, but also in colonial European theatres such as Africa and Central Asia. Theoretical rates of fire were as high as 1,200rpm, but

Did you know?

Explaining the background to his infamous gun, Richard Gatling said: 'It occurred to me that if I could invent a machine – a gun – which could by its rapidity of fire, enable one man to do as much battle duty as a hundred, that it would, to a large extent supersede the necessity of large armies, and consequently, exposure to battle and disease [would] be greatly diminished.'

practically the rate was closer to 400rpm. The biggest problem with the Gatling largely proved to be its unreliable black powder ammunition, which also produced choking and obscuring clouds of smoke when the gun was under full steam.

The Gatling was an inspiration to many, and other similar weapons emerged over the next two decades. In 1871 Benjamin Berkeley Hotchkiss from Connecticut invented a slow-firing (one round per second) five-barrelled 1.5in cannon, on first glances working on similar rotary principles to the Gatling, but actually using a single breech that fed the rounds into the barrel immediately in front of it. In 1874 the Gardner gun emerged (named after former

◄ *A French heavy-calibre Gatling-type gun of the later nineteenth century. Note the wheeled carriage – machine guns were largely treated as small artillery pieces in the early days of their use.*

The magazine Scientific American features US Army trials of an early version of the Gatling gun.

The principles of the Gatling gun have been employed in the modern M134 Minigun, an electrically powered rotary-barrel machine gun that can fire up to 6,000rpm.

Union Army captain William Gardner), a two-barrel hopper-fed design that during a test in June 1879 fired 10,000 rounds in less than 30 minutes. In the early 1890s, the Swedish Nordenfelt Volleygun had between two and 12 barrels organized in a horizontal arrangement; the two-barrel weapon had a cyclical rate of 300rpm, while the 12-barrel version technically could reach 4,000rpm. Another innovation was the Lowell Gun, so named after the Lowell Manufacturing Company of Lowell, Massachusetts, headed by DeWitt Clinton Faringdon. Development of the Lowell gun actually began back in the late 1850s, and was the brainchild of inventor C.E. Barnes. In its developed state by the 1870s, the Lowell gun consisted of a reciprocating breech block similar to the Gatling's, but had only three barrels, these

The breech block is the part of the gun responsible for sealing the breech of the gun for firing. It is also known as the bolt, although generally 'breech block' refers to a larger, more rectangular structure whereas bolt applies to more cylindrical mechanisms.

being used one at a time until heat build-up necessitated switching to another barrel. Powered once again by a cranking handle, the Lowell gun was actually a design to rival the Gatling. In a two-day test firing in 1875 the weapon went through 50,000 rounds of ammunition with only two stoppages, a feat that most modern machine guns would almost certainly fail to achieve. Commercially the Lowell gun was a failure, but some of its principles went on to inform subsequent firearms designs.

The manually operated guns were powerful in their own right, and became popular additions to land armies across North America and Europe. Yet it was evident what the weak link was – the human operator. Being operated by a handle meant that the weapons were limited by human speed and endurance, which could only be exceeded by multiplying the number of barrels and therefore dramatically increasing the cost of the weapon and the problems of ammunition feed. Yet there was a potential solution within the very principles on which firearms operated.

Whenever a gun is fired, there are two primary forces at work. First, the gas created by the burnt propellant is ejected violently forward, thrusting the bullet out of the barrel. Second, the detonation of the cartridge produces a reward recoil force against the base of the cartridge and the bolt of the gun. It would take American-born British citizen Hiram Stevens Maxim to utilise these forces to produce the world's first true machine gun.

Maxim, born in Sangerville, Maine, in 1840, had ingenuity from the outset. Working in his father's watermill, then as an apprentice carriage maker, taught him fundamental principles of engineering, and he went on to establish his own engineering company, the Maxim Gas Machine Company. By his own admission, he began toying with ideas about machine guns by the age of 14, one of his first projects being a design for a lever-operated belt-fed gun, based on a suggestion from his father. Much of his inventive energy, however, was swept into other projects, including pioneering work in electricity and its application to lighting. His development of an incandescent light bulb so threatened history's traditional inventor of the light bulb, Thomas Edison, that Edison's company even sent Maxim to Europe on a substantial salary to study European developments in lighting technology, to get him out of the way. According to legend, it was while in Vienna in 1882 that Maxim received the commercial inspiration to invest his energies in weapons design, when an acquaintance advised him: 'Hang your chemistry and electricity. If you want to make a pile of money invent something

Did you know?
Maxim was a successful general inventor rather than a gun designer per se. His inventions include a steam inhaler for people suffering chest complaints, steam pumps, a popular type of mousetrap and he is even a genuine contender for inventor of the incandescent light bulb.

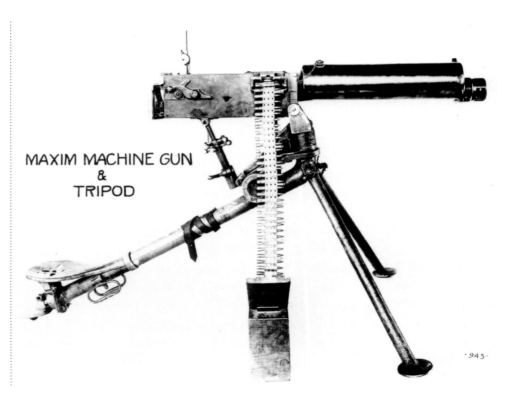

➤ An advertisement for the Maxim gun on its tripod mount. Note the fabric ammunition belt, which was fed into the gun from right to left.

MAXIM MACHINE GUN
&
TRIPOD

-943-

◄ A rather outlandish early idea for mobile firepower – fitting an air-cooled Maxim to a de Dion Bouton motorcycle, with 'armour' provided by a small frontal shield.

The temperature generated by burning propellant is around 3632°F (2000°C), and the surface of the bore (the inside of the barrel) can reach up to 1832°F (1000°C).

that will enable these Europeans to cut each other's throats with greater facility.'

Back in his mid-20s, following a bout of practise at a rifle range in Savannah, Georgia, Maxim hit on the possibility of using the force of recoil to power a gun. He was impressed by the bruise left on his shoulder by the Springfield rifle's kick, and realized that only a small proportion of the total force exerted on firing actually went into propelling the bullet. Poor ammunition meant that this insight remained just a curiosity until the 1880s, by which time powerful unitary cartridges were on the scene. Maxim now applied himself with increased vigour to utilising this force in a new weapon, working out of a London workshop. After a concentrated burst of inventiveness, in June and July 1883 Maxim was granted patents for the first machine gun design. (Maxim was extremely diligent in patenting every aspect of his design as he went along.) By the following year, he had a fully functional model ready for testing, known as the 'Prototype'. The preceding design had been the 'Forerunner', and had used cartridges designed by Maxim himself. The big difference with the 'Prototype' was that it used standard .45 Martini-Henry rimmed cartridges (as used by the British Army in their rifles), thus making itself compatible with a popular ammunition type. A test firing on the gun in January 1884 rattled through about 12 cartridges in less than a second, but barrel overheating was an immediately apparent problem. Maxim's solution was to encase most of the length of the barrel in a large water jacket, the water serving to draw off the excess heat.

➤ *The German MG08 (top) and MG08-15, the primary machine guns of Germany's land forces in World War I. The MG08-15 was a failed attempt at producing a light machine gun.*

The operating system of this new gun was revolutionary on so many levels. The fundamental principles behind Maxim's machine gun were laid out in his patent (No. 3178) of 26 June 1883, which explained that the weapon was:

> designed to utilise the kick or recoil of the rifle, or other arm, for operating the breech-loading mechanism, and constructed in such a manner that when the arm is discharged, the recoil stores up sufficient energy in a spring or springs to operate the mechanism for extracting the exploded cartridge shells, for cocking the arm, for transferring the cartridges from the magazine to the rear of the barrel, forcing them into the barrel and closing the breech.

In the 1884 design, when the gun was loaded and ready to fire (with a cartridge in the chamber) the breech block was secured up against the rear of the barrel by a hook. Upon firing, recoil forces drove the barrel and breech block back by about a half inch, at which point the hook unlatched and the breech block continued rearwards while the spent cartridge case was extracted and ejected. The breech block was attached to a flywheel crank, and eventually the energy stored in the flywheel arrested the breech block's travel and propelled it forward again. As it went forward, another cartridge was stripped out and loaded into the chamber ready for firing. Most significantly, as long as the operator kept the trigger depressed, the gun would keep firing.

Did you know?
Firearms historian Ian Hogg noted of Maxim that 'had he been so minded, he could probably have quoted one of his many patents and stifled machine gun development for the next 21 years, since almost every successful machine gun design can be foreseen in a Maxim patent.' (Hogg, *The Story of the Gun*, Boxtree, 1996)

➤ Maxim firepower travelled the globe. Here we see a tripod-mounted MG08 left on Direction Island in the Pacific, the weapons abandoned by the German Navy in 1914.

➤➤ German naval troops from SMS Königsberg in East Africa demonstrate anti-aircraft applications of the Maxim, finding a novel method of achieving elevation.

Did you know?

There are two types of recoil operation. Short recoil means the barrel and bolt unlock after a very short distance of travel backwards, while in long recoil they unlock once they have covered more than the distance of the unfired cartridge.

Maxim was on the verge of creating a weapon that would change the face of warfare, but there were a few refinements to come. A demonstration in January 1885 in front of senior British military observers, including the Commander-in-Chief of the British Army, Lord Wolseley, the Duke of Cambridge, and Lieutenant-General Sir Andrew Clarke, the Inspector General of Fortifications, produced a list of recommended improvements, including simplifying and lightening the design, and creating a weapon that could be field serviced without the need for special tools. Maxim went back to the drawing board. The new design that emerged later in the year changed the internal workings of the gun quite substantially, although recoil still provided the motive power. In the new gun, the flywheel mechanism was removed and

the breech block movement was controlled by a hinged arm known as a toggle lock. When the arm was straight, it was locked and held the breech block firmly up against the barrel. As with the previous weapon, on firing the breech block and barrel recoiled together for about half an inch, but at that point the toggle lock was 'broken' at the hinge joint by a roller, allowing the breech to continue rearwards while the barrel returned to its firing position. (Note that the half inch distance of locked travel was necessary to allow the pressures in the gun to drop to safe levels before the breech block and barrel separated.) With extraction and ejection performed, spring power then returned the whole mechanism to its original position, the toggle lock snapping back into its rigid original configuration for firing the next cartridge.

➤ *Despite its powerful 8 x 56R Austrian Mannlicher rifle cartridge, the Austrian Schwarzlose machine gun (here seen during a night firing) used a blowback design. It worked well nonetheless, and was used by several European armies.*

➤➤ *An Austrian battalion man a Maxim gun in Italy, 1917. The Maxim was an extremely heavy gun to transport and handle in mountainous terrain.*

The new design was the final critical step in the design of the first effective service machine gun. Such was its durability and reliability that machine guns based directly on this operating principle would still be in either production or service after World War II. First, however, Maxim had to translate a successful design into a commercial reality. Maxim embarked on a tireless marketing campaign around Europe. One favoured demonstration technique was to use the Maxim to cut down a substantial tree just by firepower alone. Military observers were undoubtedly impressed (although many were more than a little concerned about the potential costs of ammunition), and orders began to flood in. By the end of the 1880s the Maxim Gun Company (as the new company was called) was supplying machine guns to Austria, Britain, Germany Italy, Switzerland and Austria.

Maxim's weapon offered terrible new battlefield capabilities. Here was a weapon that could fire hundreds of rifle-calibre bullets every minute, each round having a lethal range of more than a mile. Fire could be directed either at a 'point target' (a single, identifiable target such as a bunker) or used more generally against an 'area target', such as a trench system or troops advancing across open ground. The machine gun created a lethal 'beaten zone', an elliptical area defined by the moment a bullet would first catch a standing human to the point at which the bullet struck the ground. Anyone within the beaten zone, which could be hundreds of yards long depending on the angle of fire, was likely to be hit if they were not behind very substantial cover.

Did you know?
The Maxim Gun had a cyclical rate of fire of about 600rpm. It would take 40 contemporary rifle-armed infantrymen to produce the same amount of firepower over a 60-second period.

◄◄ *A Montenegrin machine gun battery deploy two Maxim guns during World War I. Note the empty fabric feed belt emerging from the nearest gun; cartridges were stripped from the belt and fired as they passed through the gun.*

Soon the Maxim, in its various production models, had its first combat testing. On 21 November 1888, a single Maxim in British hands utterly crushed a tribal uprising in Sierra Leone. (The British actually officially adopted the Maxim the following year, and opted to change its calibre to .303 instead of .45.) More British Maxims were used in earnest in North Transvaal, South Africa, during the Matabele War of 1893–94. In one notable, vicious action, 50 British infantrymen armed with four Maxims slaughtered almost to a man 5,000 Matabele warriors in a 90-minute battle.

In Europe's various colonial wars, the Maxim was proving its grim worth as a new tool of warfare. And yet even as the Maxim was establishing itself, new types of machine gun were emerging.

Recoil-operated machine guns are still very much in production and service to this day, yet they are only one of three basic types of automatic mechanism. The two others are blowback and gas. In a blowback-operated weapon, the bolt is not locked to the barrel when the gun is fired – it is held in place purely by the force of the return spring (the spring that returns the breech block to the firing position). Firing

◄ The Colt Model 1895 'Potato Digger', the first operational gas-operated machine gun, was used by the US Navy, US Marines and US Army, as well as by Spanish, British and Italian forces.

imparts recoil forces to the now empty cartridge case, which literally pushes back the bolt against a return spring to perform the cycle of ejection then reloading. Because the bolt is not locked, blowback is generally only suited to low-powered cartridges (such as the pistol cartridges used in submachine guns), although this did not stop some early designers creating full-blown machine guns on the blowback principle. In 1888, the Austrians Archduke Karl Salvatore and Lieutenant Ritter von Dormus took out a patent for a blowback-operated machine gun, which subsequently became the Model 1893, better known as the Skoda machine gun after the name of its manufacturer. Strictly speaking, the Skoda machine gun worked on a system of delayed blowback – the backwards movement of the bolt was momentarily delayed by mechanical means to allow the breech pressure to drop to safe levels before the breech opened. The Skoda went through several versions and served in World War I, and although reliable, its use of weaker 8 x 50R Mannlicher service cartridges meant that it was largely obsolete by the time the war started in 1914.

A far more important operating mechanism in machine guns is gas operation. Gas-operated guns, as the name describes, utilise the gas produced by the burnt propellant to cycle the gun. The pioneer in this regard was the legendary firearms designer John Moses Browning. Having cut his teeth on rifles and shotguns, Browning attempted a machine gun in the late 1880s. The initial design featured a blast-catching metal plate just behind the muzzle, the firing gases striking the plate

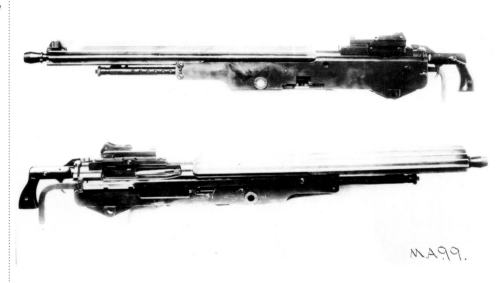

> The .30 Marlin M1918 was a much improved variation of the Colt M1885, which did away with the swinging arm gas system in favour of a straightforward gas cylinder. It was used in infantry, armoured and aviation units.

M.A.99.

and, via various mechanical attachments, forcing back the breech to allow ejection then reloading. The design was a clattering affair, however, so he refined it by drilling a hole in the barrel's underside, this forming a gas port that powered a hinged operating arm beneath the barrel. The hacking action of the lever led to the gun being branded as the Colt M1895 'Potato Digger', and it subsequently entered service with the US Navy, Army and Marine Corps, who all appreciated its 400+rpm performance.

◄ *British troops using a Colt M1895. Aiming is via a ladder-rack sight at the rear of the gun, this providing a simple guide to elevation when engaging long-range targets.*

➤ *USMC troops fire a Hotchkiss Mle 1909, a French-designed 8mm gas-operated light machine gun. It had a cyclical rate of fire of around 600rpm.*

The M1895 was history's first belt-fed gas-operated machine gun, but being such an early design it had more than its fair share of problems. It had a tendency to overheat, which could result in the machine gunner's nightmare of 'cook off' (cartridges firing purely from excessive barrel heat). Yet others were also experimenting with the gas-operated model. In 1893, an Austrian Army captain, Adolf von Odkolek, produced a design for a new machine gun and offered it to the French Hotchkiss company, then run by the American Lawrence V. Bénét. Instead of Browning's lever beneath the barrel, von Odkolek had a cylinder containing a piston. When the gun was fired, gases were tapped off via a port near the muzzle and expanded inside the cylinder, impinging on the piston head and forcing it backwards. The piston was linked to the bolt by an operating rod,

and the rearward-travelling operating rod unlocked the bolt to allow ejection. The bolt then returned to the loaded position under the pressure of a return spring. Feed was via a 20-round metal strip.

While Browning was the leader in the field of gas-operated machine guns (although Maxim himself had sketched out some designs a few years previously), it was the Hotchkiss machine gun that established the basic principles upon which gas-operated machine guns work today. The cylinder and piston arrangement is still seen in modern weapons such as the M249 Squad Automatic Weapon or the FN MAG. The principal advantages of the gas-operated system, as opposed to recoil operation, were its lightness and the controlled recoil (the gas mechanism absorbs much of the felt recoil), qualities that made it especially

Did you know?

The 'Potato Digger', nickname of the Colt M1895, had an almost literal origin. If the underneath of the gun was too close to the ground when the weapon was being fired, the operating lever could literally chop its way into the ground.

➤ *The Hotchkiss Mle 1909, seen here in USMC hands in Nicaragua in 1912, was fed by 24- or 30-round metallic cartridge strips, supported by the gunner's assistant to the right of the gunner.*

➤➤ *The Hotchkiss Mle 1914, here seen on its tripod mount, was the fourth in the series of Hotchkiss gas-operated guns. The observer at the rear looks out for potential targets.*

41

◀ Soldiers of the Indian Army prepare to fire their gas-operated Lewis guns. The Lewis had a 550rpm rate of fire, from a distinctive 47-round pan magazine.

◀◀ The Hotchkiss Mle 1914 was used heavily by the American Expeditionary Force (AEF) in 1917 and 1918, America's entry into World War I having revealed a shortage of indigenous machine guns.

suited to the future light machine gun (LMG) designs (see chapter on Light and Aviation Machine Guns). Gas-operated guns can also fire much faster than recoil-operated weapons. The disadvantages are, however, the greater mechanical complexity and also the inevitable issues with fouling. Propellant gas is dirty stuff, and during prolonged firing carbon build-up in gas ports and other parts steadily makes it harder for the gun to perform its cycle. Throughout history this problem has been managed by fitting gas regulator devices, systems that either increase or maintain the flow of gas into the piston, but there is no denying that even today gas-operated guns need meticulous and regular cleaning to keep working smoothly. Recoil-operated weapons have sealed barrels, so the propellant gases don't work their way back into the operating mechanism.

By the beginning of the twentieth century, machine guns had become accepted elements of the global military arsenal, in either recoil-, gas- or blowback-operated formats. Now came a period of development, in which militarized nations sought to produce new models with greater battle efficiency. These models emerged at a formative period in the machine gun's history, and while some neared combat perfection, others were simply dreadful. The French went though a rapid sequence of Hotchkiss variations, which were more or less serviceable, but also produced the shockingly unreliable 8mm Puteaux Modèle (Mle) 1905 and the equally disastrous 8mm Saint-Etienne Mle 1907. The Austrians persisted down the blowback route, and from 1905 produced the 8mm Schwarzlose machine gun. Despite using blowback with powerful 8 x 56R Mannlicher rifle rounds, the Schwarzlose was actually a decent weapon, and served outside of Austria in German, Greek, Dutch, Hungarian and Italian armies.

Other nations, by contrast, simply adapted the Maxim gun to their own needs. The Germans produced the 7.92mm MG08, essentially a Maxim gun mounted

◀ *The Vickers machine gun was arguably the finest manifestation of Maxim gun principles. With devastating long-range firepower and total dependability, the Vickers transformed British firepower.*

▶ During World War I, machine guns were increasingly applied to anti-aircraft roles. Here we see French troops with a Hotchkiss Mle 1914 on a swivel anti-aircraft mount.

▶▶ A Vickers machine gun team receive instruction in the correct loading procedure. The tube descending from the muzzle typically connected to a steam condensing tank, used to collect water that evaporated from the water jacket.

on a variety of home-grown tripods and carriages. The British also went down this route, and in so doing created one of the finest machine guns of all time. Taking the Maxim, the engineers of Vickers, Son and Maxim Ltd modified the mechanism slightly (the main change was making the toggle lock break upwards instead of downwards) to reduce the size of the receiver. The .303 Vickers Mk I machine gun was introduced into service in November 1912, and although it went through several variations, it was largely the same gun when it was retired from British service in the 1960s; other nations continued to use it into the 1980s and beyond. A water-cooled weapon fed by 250-round fabric belts, the Vickers could keep up a steady 450rpm of fire with legendary reliability. On one occasion during World War I, 10 Vickers of the 100th Company of the Machine Gun Corps fired for 12 hours straight, in the process burning through a million rounds of ammunition and 100 barrels, but never breaking down. It was the sort of reliability on which soldiers could hang their lives, and as such it was a much respected gun.

The battlefields of World War I were indeed the true proving ground of machine guns on both tactical and technological levels, although earlier conflicts such as the Russo-Japanese War of 1904–05 laid the foundations, with impressive use of machine guns on both sides. This is not to say, however, that machine guns were universally appreciated at the beginning of the war. In Britain, for example, production quotas of machine guns were initially extremely low (there were only about 200 machine guns in British Army service at the

◄◄ Machine guns were applied as primary weapons to early light tanks and armoured cars. Here a Hotchkiss machine gun is mounted in a French Renault FT-17 tank.

➤ *Tactically, MGs were ideally suited to static trench defence, providing commanding firepower over open land. Here a French machine gun team post guard over a stretch of road.*

An experimental British machine gun configuration, with a Vickers mounted on the back of a small flat-bed truck. In practical usage across uneven land, this arrangement would be largely impractical.

➤ A British Vickers team fighting on the Somme in 1916. Firing accurately while wearing the visually restrictive gas hoods can't have been easy.

outbreak of war), primarily because the commanders expected a war of movement, and the bulky machine guns were not terribly mobile. There was also a cultural problem in that to many the machine gun seemed somewhat 'ungentlemanly', a form of weaponry that subordinated the warrior spirit to industrial, grinding firepower.

During the early part of the war, British machine guns were generally issued around two per battalion of infantry, and they were used unintelligently – often wheeled about like miniature artillery pieces, in which unsuitable role their crews became open targets for enemy riflemen. It was the Germans who began to show the Allies what the machine guns could really do, particularly once the war had frozen into largely static trench lines on the Western Front. Trench warfare was less about movement and more about attrition, and machine guns could do the latter with ghastly ease. The Germans pushed as many machine guns into the frontlines as possible, keeping few in reserve, and positioned them with interlocking fields of fire across terrain made more challenging by barbed-wire defences. Attacking British infantry were slowed by the barbed wire, and cut down like chaff under rattling hails of fire.

The Allies, locked into an offensive mindset, were slow to realize that the machine gun had changed the nature of warfare itself. The cost was terrible. During Allied offensives at Neuve Chapelle in March 1915, Loos in the following September and at the Somme in July 1916, there were several cases of one or two German machine guns decimating

Did you know?
Within two months of the outbreak of World War I in June 1914, the Germans had more than 10,000 machine guns in service. By the end of the war they had more than 100,000 such weapons.

➤ World War I stocks of weaponry were often pressed into service in the early years of World War II. Here a German soldier in Poland, September 1939, mans an MG08-15.

entire battalions of British infantry, the German gunners doing little more than keeping the guns fed with ammunition and traversing them across the British lines. At the Somme, the Germans also demonstrated their ability to deploy the machine guns rapidly from deep dugouts to the rear, where the gunners had sat out the initial British preparatory bombardment in relative safety.

Finally, the penny dropped on the British side, as they realized that machine guns and artillery were now kings of the battlefield, not the individual soldier clutching his bolt-action rifle. The military historian James Willbanks explains the change in the way the Allies deployed their machine guns:

The belligerents realized that with the machine gun dominating the battlefield, they would need many more such weapons. When war started, the general allocation of machine guns on the Allied side was some 24 guns per division of 12 battalions. By the end, the divisions had been pared to nine battalions, but the number of machine guns had increased to 160.

(James H. Willbanks, *Machine guns: an illustrated history of their impact*: ABC-CLIO, 2004, p.68)

Once the Allies bought into the machine-gun age, then the Germans began to experience the scything firepower they had inflicted at so many battles. In addition, the roles of machine guns themselves were becoming much broader than previously conceived.

Although there was no doubt about the capability of the heavy machine guns (HMGs) – machine guns designed to be fired from tripods or similar mounts in a sustained-fire role – they had some serious battlefield limitations. Chief amongst the problems was their sheer weight. The German MG08, for example, totalled 137lb (62kg) if its carriage and spare parts were included, an enormous weight to haul through the mud of a battlefield. Such weight was fine if the gun was emplaced in a static defensive position, but as soon as you wanted to move, it became a heavy

➤ US troops man a Chauchat Mle 1915, widely regarded as history's worst machine gun. Note the highly unreliable semi-circular magazine, which had open sides and freely let dirt enter the mechanism.

◄ French and colonial troops occupying a trench in May 1914. The composition of firepower is typical – a section of riflemen with a machine gun (here a Chauchat) in support.

57

➤ A Japanese machine gun team in China covers an infantry advance with a 6.5mm Taisho 3rd Year gun. Produced from 1914, the 3rd Year was essentially a Hotchkiss copy with heavy barrel finning to disperse barrel heat.

➤➤ An unusual shot of German soldiers in Italy in October 1917 armed with captured stocks of Allied Lewis guns, which were far better LMGs than anything in German stocks at that time.

burden indeed. What was needed, quite literally, was a light machine gun, a gun that could be moved easily by attacking infantry to provide on-the-spot heavy firepower.

Development of what became known as the LMG class actually predated the war. The first significant production LMG came from Denmark in the very first years of the twentieth century. The Madsen was a recoil-operated gun, but it was in no way a standard design. It had a fiendishly complicated action, which involved the bolt performing its usual duties of closing the breech and firing, but with separate mechanisms doing all the other work of extracting and reloading. Nevertheless, it worked superbly and, firing from 25-, 30- or 40-round box magazines, was highly portable – the empty, bipod-mounted gun weighed only 20lb (9kg). It was

◀ A British Lewis gunner takes aim over the parapet of his trench on the Somme battlefield, July 1916. The Lewis was portable enough to be carried across the battlefield in the assault phase.

◀◀ Here enterprising British gunners have mounted a Lewis gun on a carriage wheel and axle, producing an improvised form of anti-aircraft gun.

combat tested by Russian cavalry during the Russo-Japanese War of 1904–05, and demonstrated the value of having a machine gun that could be taken with soldiers on the advance.

In the run-up to and early years of World War I, other nations pursued the LMG ideal. The French and the Germans both tried to create LMGs from their existing types, the Germans having little success while the French produced the Hotchkiss Mle 1909, a rather awkward weapon that was still a little too heavy for true battlefield mobility. The French also designed the 8mm Chauchat Mle 1915, which is widely regarded as history's worst machine gun. Although intended as an LMG, the Chauchat used a long-recoil system – the barrel and bolt recoiled for more than the length of the entire

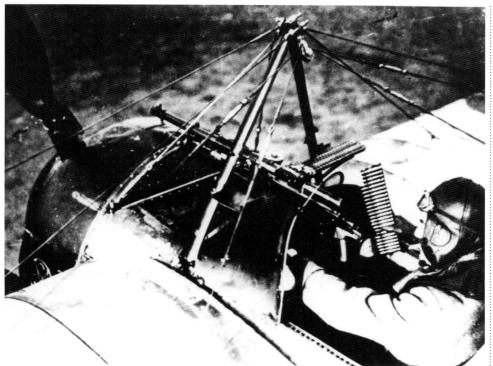

◄ This French Morane-Saulnier Type N fighter has been fitted with a Hotchkiss M1909 machine gun, which has been set to fire through the propeller. Note the awkward reloading arrangement – flying and reloading at the same time must have been a feat of dexterity.

cartridge before being unlocked to enable ejection and reloading. The result was a shuddering experience for the gunner, which combined with poor ammunition, a badly designed semi-circular magazine, and inferior construction materials led to constant jams and breakages.

A far more successful LMG came from the United States courtesy of Colonel (US Army) Isaac Newton Lewis. Taking an earlier design for a light, gas-operated machine gun, Lewis developed what became known to posterity as the Lewis gun. Light at 26lb (11.8kg), and fed by a 47-round flat pan magazine mounted on the top of the action, the gas-operated Lewis could fire at 550rpm. It had a large, distinctive metal tube wrapped around the barrel. This tube encased a finned radiator that actually sucked cooling air into the rear of the tube when the gun fired (utilising the suction created by the muzzle blast), which helped in cooling the barrel.

Although the Lewis was a US weapon, it was primarily adopted and manufactured in Europe, probably on account of personal rivalries between Lewis and the authorities in the US Ordnance Corps. The British were especially wedded to the Lewis, and during World War I it excelled as a one-gunner weapon, providing mobile firepower during assault operations. The Lewis also took on new life aboard early combat aircraft – indeed, air forces would become major customers for machine gun technology in general over the next decades. Early applications of machine guns to biplane fighters and bombers worked simply by mounting the machine gun either on a separate pintle mount for the co-pilot/

observer/gunner to operate (in an aircraft with two crew members) or by clamping it to a fixed mount on the top wing, shooting clear of the propellers out front. Both arrangements were unsatisfactory, the former because of the risk of a gunner shooting up his own plane in the twists and turns of a dogfight, the latter because the fighter pilot struggled to aim a gun accurately that wasn't aligned directly with his eyeline. A partial, if slightly hair-raising solution came from Frenchman Roland Garros in December 1914. Garros, in cooperation with the Morane-Saulnier aviation company, developed metal deflector plates attached to the propeller blades. A Lewis gun was then mounted on the engine cowling of a Morane-Saulnier Type L aircraft, the machine gun positioned in front of the pilot and firing directly through the propeller blades. The idea was simple – by mounting the machine gun in front of the pilot, the pilot could aim directly down the gun barrel using an optical sight; most of the bullets fired passed between the propeller blades, and those that struck would be deflected by the metal shields.

The idea sounds impractical but it worked, and Garros shot down three German aircraft with the system in April 1915. The Germans were initially alarmed and mystified by the aircraft losses, but the mystery was revealed when Garros' plane was shot down over German lines. Instead of simply copying the Garros mechanism, however, the Germans made a seminal leap forward. The aircraft designer Anthony Fokker developed a 'synchroniser gear', a mechanical linkage between the engine and the firing mechanism that only permitted the gun to fire when the propeller blades were clear of the shot. Allied to a fresh German machine gun, the 1911 Parabellum, two of which were mounted on the German fighters, the synchroniser gear changed the face of air combat. The fighter aircraft was born, and soon the Allies had developed their own synchroniser systems, mounting modified twin Vickers machines. The skies over the war zones were quickly filled with twisting aerial dogfights, each pilot attempting to bring his machine guns to bear on the evasive target.

Although the Lewis gun did not achieve a high status in its country of origin, once the United States entered the war in 1917 American firearms designers stepped up to the mark. In fact, the US machine guns designed during the last years of World War I and the inter-war years remain some of the greatest machine guns in history, with certain models in service with the US and international forces today in largely unmodified form. The name that hangs over them all is Browning. In 1917, Browning demonstrated a gun that actually had been designed about seven years previously. The .30 Browning M1917, as it was known in its first incarnation, was a belt-fed, recoil-operated gun of similar appearance to the Maxim – its barrel was wrapped in a large water jacket.

◀ US troops of late World War I set up the rear ladder sight of a Browning .30 M1917 machine gun. The 250-round fabric ammunition belt is fed from an ammunition box to the side.

Did you know?

During a trial of the Browning M1917 in May 1917, the gun fired 40,000 rounds with only two stoppages and no breakages. Even the stoppages were the fault of the ammunition, not the gun.

➤ The Browning M1917 was widely exported. Here Chinese communist troops operate such a weapon during fighting with Nationalists in China in the late 1940s.

The M1917 was everything a machine gun should be, and it would stay in US service in subsequent versions until the present day. Versions produced included the M1918 air-cooled aviation gun and various weapons for armoured vehicle mounts. Yet by far the most famous offshoot was the M1919 version (itself divided into several sub-varieties). Here Browning dispensed altogether with the water jacket to create an air-cooled weapon distinguished by an instantly recognisable slotted barrel jacket. The M1919A4 and A6 versions became the classic models, the dominant medium machine gun (MMG) type throughout World War II and for many years beyond. Other varieties were designed specifically for vehicle, aircraft or naval use.

But Browning's M1917 and M1919 guns were just one part of his prodigious creative output around this time. Also in 1917, Browning began production of an LMG, or heavy automatic rifle, depending on how you bend the definition. The .30 Browning Automatic Rifle M1918 – better known as the 'BAR' (with each letter pronounced) – was an unusual weapon, being essentially a heavy-barrelled gas-operated automatic rifle with a bipod mount, and firing from a 20-round box magazine. The BAR was

Did you know?

In modern use, a heavy machine gun is a weapon firing full-power rifle cartridges or bullets up to .50in (12.7mm) from substantial tripods or other mounts, and capable of sustained fire. A medium machine gun also fires rifle rounds, but can be used from either a bipod or a tripod and offers greater portability. A light machine gun is easily handled by one person, but is generally only suited to controlled burst fire, not sustained fire, from a bipod.

► Norwegian troops man a Browning M1919. The actual operating mechanism of the Browning was designed back in 1910, but it took several years to interest the US authorities in its possibilities.

►► US troops at the end of World War I practise on the range with the Browning Automatic Rifle (BAR). Gunner's assistants stand by with additional 20-round box magazines.

➤➤ *The Browning M1919A4 was one of the best medium machine guns of World War II and beyond. It was a .30-calibre weapon fired at a controllable cyclical rate of 500rpm.*

oddly positioned – too heavy to be a standard rifle, yet basically too light to cope with the recoil forces of full-auto fire. (It weighed 16lb/7.3kg.) Its 20-round magazine emptied too quickly at the 500rpm cyclical rate to provide any sort of prolonged fire support. Yet the weapon became a hit, and more than 52,000 were produced by war's end, and many more beyond.

As World War I drew to a close, Browning also designed a gun of even greater historical status than the BAR. Prompted by official requests for a HMG capable of engaging aircraft, observation balloons and protected land targets, Browning came up with the M1921. This was a water-cooled weapon firing the potent .50-calibre round, an ammunition type with exceptional range and penetration. The M1921 and subsequent (1930) M1921A1

worked well, and an air-cooled M2 version was also produced, principally for aviation applications. The M2 had the advantage of weight reduction, but firing the heavy slugs meant that anything approaching sustained fire resulted in the barrel overheating. John Browning was by now dead (he passed away in 1926), but development of his gun continued and yielded the M2HB, the 'HB' letters standing for 'Heavy Barrel'. This was largely the same gun, but fitted with a thick barrel better suited to soaking up the intense heat generated by firing. The M2HB is still seen today in the hands of armies around the world, typically mounted on vehicles – total empty weight is around 84lb (38kg). A quick-change barrel (QCB) version introduced in the 1970s by the Belgian company Fabrique Nationale prolonged its shelf life even further. What

Did you know?
Fabrique Nationale
Herstal (FN Herstal)
is one of the world's
oldest and most
successful weapons
manufacturers.
Originally known as
Fabrique National
d'Armes de Guerre, this
Belgian company was
founded in 1889 and
from 1897 developed
a close relationship
with Browning. Today
Browning is an
FN subsidiary.

keeps the M2HB in use is its formidable destructive force (there are few structures in an urban environment that can stop its firepower), its long range (well in excess of a mile) and its day-after-day reliability.

Browning's guns would provide US forces with its machine gun needs during the inter-war years, and in the world war to come.

Yet other nations around the world did not stand still during the 1920s and 1930s. The inter-war years were a time of tactical reappraisal in many of the world's armies. The armies of Europe and the United States were becoming increasingly mechanized (at least in thought if not in reality), and the tactical focus shifted to mobility and

➤ A water-cooled .50 Browning M2. The tubes looping out of the water jacket allowed for the constant circulation of cooling fluid through the jacket.

➤➤ The ultimate evolution of the Browning .50 M2, the M2HB, featured an extremely substantial barrel better suited to coping with the harsh temperatures generated by the potent .50 rounds.

➤ *The Czechs were at the forefront of LMG design during the inter-war years. The gas-operated 7.92mm ZB26 was manufactured by the Brno Arms Factory, and laid the groundwork for the British Bren gun.*

◄ *The ZB30 was an improved version of the earlier ZB26. It was not only a direct forerunner of the British Bren, but it was even produced by the Germans during World War II and by several other nations after the war.*

Most medium and heavy machine guns have a barrel-change facility. The frequency with which a barrel is changed depends on the rate of fire of the gun and how many rounds are fired per minute. A gunner firing frequent but short bursts might only have to change the barrel every half hour, whereas rapid sustained fire might necessitate a barrel change every five or 10 minutes.

manoeuvre rather than simply attrition. The infantry had to be more capable of taking their firepower with them, so much investment went into creating fresh LMG types. The Czechs, for example, produced the ZB26 and ZB30 LMGs, both gas-operated types with curved, top-mounted 30-round box magazines and front bipods, with barrel handles facilitating both carrying and the barrel-change process. They were excellent guns, so much so that Britain essentially borrowed the design and, modifying it to fire the British standard .303 round, created the famous Bren gun in the early 1930s. The Bren was a superlative LMG – accurate, reliable, easy to control – and would stay in service in the L4 7.62mm NATO version until the 1980s.

Other nations brought out their own new batch of LMGs. France produced an updated series of Hotchkiss guns between 1922 and 1926, although they saw limited service use, and several models of 7.5mm Châtellerault machine gun, which was in its action indebted to the American BAR, although using a top-loading magazine. The Châtellerault finally gave the French a decent LMG, and put the curse of the Chauchat largely behind them. Italy manufactured a range of light, medium and heavy machine guns made variously by Breda, Scotti and Fiat-Revelli, all tending to be a little more complex than they needed to be (a characteristic of many early Italian automatic weapons).

The Russians were also busy at the drawing board. The main machine gun in the Russian arsenal until the late 1920s was the 7.62mm Maxim M1910, a hefty piece mounted on its own wheeled carriage.

◄ The MG13 was an interwar German LMG. It was a decent enough weapon, but during the 1930s it was superseded by the illustrious MG34, and most MG13s were sold off to Portugal.

Attempts to lighten the design to create a dedicated LMG were not successful, but in 1928 the Red Army purchased a new weapon, the redoubtable 7.62mm Degtyarev DP. Recognised by its distinctive 47-shot flat pan magazine on the top – actually the gun's only weak element – the DP was a typically robust Soviet affair, and gave generally reliable performance whatever the elements or conditions.

➤ *Italian soldiers demonstrate a 12.7mm Breda 37 machine gun to German military personnel. The Breda was a gas-operated machine gun that was originally designed as a tank weapon.*

◄ *The Italian Breda Model 30 was a blowback-operated machine gun. It had a fixed magazine, this hinging forward for loading with rifle chargers.*

It also yielded a tank- and vehicle-mounted variant, the Degtyarev DT.

Meanwhile, Germany was taking a steady evolutionary path to excellence in its machine gun designs. Maxim guns and their variants had served the Germans well in terms of HMGs, but there were failed attempts to turn the Maxim into an LMG variant. However, in 1917 engineer Carl Gast designed the air-cooled, twin-barrelled 7.92mm Gast gun, intended for aviation use. Together, the twin barrels could pump out 1300rpm, but although the weapon was decent it was produced in only tiny numbers, and largely kept secret. Germany brought out other light, air-cooled machine guns during the 1920s and early 1930s however, such as the MG13, MG15 and MG30, and it was this series of guns that led to the MG34, a world-class machine gun. The MG34 was light at only 26.67lb (12.10kg), but it could gobble through 7.92mm rounds at 900rpm, 400rpm faster than a Bren or the Browning M1919. It was fed from either a 75-round saddle drum magazine, or a 250-shot belt, making it a new class of machine gun – the general-purpose machine gun (GPMG). The GPMG could switch between roles depending on its configuration. With the drum magazine and a bipod, it was a true LMG. (During the war, the drum was rarely used, the firepower of the belt being preferred.) With bipod/light tripod and belt feed it served as an MMG. Put it on a heavy tripod, and you essentially had an HMG suited to sustained fire. The MG34 was a taste of things to come, and for the Allies who faced such weapons during World War II, the taste was very bitter indeed.

➤➤ British soldiers receive instruction on the Besa, a heavy 7.92mm machine gun designed from the Czech ZB53 for use in British tanks and armoured cars. It was an accurate and generally reliable weapon.

Although, as we shall see, there were some important developments in machine gun technology during World War II, most of the engineering groundwork was laid before the conflict began. For that reason, World War II's relationship with the machine gun was more about refinements at the tactical level, rather than pushing new boundaries in terms of design.

An exception to this rule was the development of a new machine gun in Germany, as German engineers sought a less expensive alternative to the industrially intensive MG34. The result was arguably the best all-round GPMG of all time – the MG42. Like the MG34, the MG42 was a recoil-operated weapon, but it took the rate of fire up to a blistering 1,200rpm. It used an innovative bolt arrangement in which the bolt was locked for firing by two rollers that cammed out into recesses in the gun's receiver, the rollers being unlocked when the gun fired by the rearward travel of the striker assembly (the unit that holds the firing pin). The mechanism allowed for the gun's fast rate of fire, and problems with overheating were handled by a true quick-change barrel facility – a barrel change could be performed in less than five seconds. The MG42 was a superb gun, of which around 400,000 were produced during the war. It could fit into a variety of roles, from light assault machine gun through to anti-aircraft weapon. Its distinctive rasping sound was notorious amongst Allied soldiers, who grew to fear meeting the MG42 in action, where it typically inflicted heavy casualties. Such was its quality that after the war, when the German Federal Army was searching for a

➤ A Finnish gunner engages enemy forces with a 7.62mm Lahti-Saloranta M26. It was designed in 1926, and was a recoil-operated gun with selective fire – it could fire either single shots or on full-auto.

◄ Strictly speaking, the FG42 was a gas-operated automatic rifle, a cutting-edge design intended primarily for German parachute forces. Mounted on a bipod, however, it served as a decent LMG.

►► *The superlative MG34 was designed by Mauser-Werke AG. Its virtues were its heavy 900rpm rate of fire, its reliability and its ability to shift between various roles.*

Did you know?

Allied soldiers came up with numerous nicknames for the MG42. They included 'linoleum ripper' (alluding to its sound), 'Hitler's zipper' and 'Hitler's buzzsaw'. The Germans themselves called it the *Hitlersäge* ('Hitler's saw').

new machine gun, it simply put a slightly modified version of the MG42 (known as the MG3) back into production, where it remains today.

Machine guns were applied to infantry warfare according to various squad, platoon, company and battalion doctrines. Unlike World War I, the infantry now integrated machine guns at every tactical level, the authorities recognizing that whoever dominated in the exchange of fire, also had greater freedom to manoeuvre. In squad and platoon offensive actions, light and medium machine guns moved with the riflemen into the attack and established bases of fire to suppress enemy abilities to manoeuvre or to fire back, thus giving the riflemen more freedom to put themselves into flanking positions, and reduce casualties in the case of a

frontal attack. German infantry manuals from the early 1940s typically have an LMG gunner as part of every squad manoeuvre, often in the vanguard of an advance or attack. US policy was similar. A US eight-man patrol formation, for example, would usually include a BAR gunner positioned on the flanks, with another man acting as an assistant to the gunner (supplying ammunition, providing cover etc). A British section (between seven and 12 men) would, similarly, include a two-man Bren team to act as the support element to the riflemen.

On the defensive, machine guns were typically sited in fixed positions, such as trenches, dug-outs and bunkers. As machine guns tend to attract a lot of enemy fire, the machine gun positions were often heavily camouflaged and protected by thick earth, log or even ferro-concrete cover. For

➤ A German MG34 emplacement on the Atlantic Wall. It was such positions that had a devastating effect on US troops at Omaha Beach, Normandy, on 6 June 1944, D-Day.

Did you know?

During World War II the US Army developed an anti-aircraft weapon system consisting of four M2HB .50-cal machine guns arranged in a single mount. The combined cyclical rate of fire was more than 2,000rpm.

urban defence, windows and door openings acted as fire apertures for the machine gunner, although he would actually site the machine gun well back inside the room – positioning himself directly in an open window created a conveniently silhouetted target for enemy snipers. Soldiers piled up furniture around the aperture to provide additional protection.

At platoon, company and battalion levels, the machine guns provided support fire alongside other infantry support weapons

such as mortars, often at long ranges and against area targets. Long-range shooting was a particular challenge, as the gunner not only had to judge the rise and fall of the bullets (hence affecting the elevation or depression of the gun), but also factor in elements such as wind speed and temperature, all of which would affect the point of impact. Support actions also required expert coordination both to synchronize the fire with the broader operational timetable, and ensure that the

➤ US Marines on Iwo Jima in February 1945 put a Japanese 7.7mm Type 92 machine gun into use. The gun was known by the Allies as the 'Woodpecker', on account of the sound made by its slow rate of fire (450rpm).

Did you know?

A 'cyclical rate of fire' refers to a gun's theoretical rate of fire if it could shoot constantly without interruption. The 'practical rate of fire', however, refers to the actual realistic rate of fire when factors such as ammunition supply, barrel heating and tactical considerations come into play.

machine gunner didn't fire upon his own people. An impression of the complexities of support fire planning come from the 1944 US Army Rifle Company manual:

As a general rule, most effective results are obtained by the simultaneous concentration of the fire of both guns on the same target. The section leader, in conformity with the platoon

A British Special Air Service (SAS) team in North Africa display vehicles bristling with Vickers K machine guns.

This US .50 quad Browning anti-aircraft gun could be pressed into service, when necessary, in a ground-support role, with devastating effect on unprotected infantry.

leader's orders, designates the targets, specifies the rate of the fire, and gives the command or signal for opening fire... When squads have been assigned sectors of fire, each squad leader takes, as his primary mission, fire on targets developing in his own sector, and as a secondary mission, fire on those targets developing in the adjacent sector. When the squad leader acts entirely on his own initiative, he decides how he can best support the general plan of the company and leads his squad accordingly.

The establishment of fire sectors was always important, as they not only ensured that the guns delivered coordinated fire on the same target, but also prevented the gunners from overswinging their muzzles and hitting nearby friendly infantry or positions. Typical practical rates of fire ranged from about 120rpm for light machine guns, through to around 350rpm for the heavier weapons.

The weapons delivering fire support naturally varied according to the army. For the British, the Bren generally served for most duties, although by 1944 infantry divisions also included a machine gun battalion, which was equipped with a heavy mortar company and three Vickers machine gun companies. A US battalion had a heavy weapons company, which consisted of two Browning .30 machine guns on tripod mounts and an 81mm mortar platoon. The .30 machine guns could also be used from bipod mounts for MMG work, alongside BARs. On the German side, MG34s and MG42s covered all roles from light support through to anti-aircraft fire, and by 1944 every

German division included a heavy weapons company, within which was a machine gun platoon with six machine guns.

Machine guns were utterly central to the infantry tactics of World War II, and they took a ghastly toll of human lives on all fronts. One British soldier, a Private Evans of the 1st Royal Norfolks, recounted how an advance in Normandy was decisively stopped by German machine guns:

So far we had covered two or three miles and were doing well until we came to a cornfield. Then Jerry machine guns in a small pillbox opened up. The lads were soon cut to pieces as the machine guns, with their tremendous rate of fire, scythed through the three-foot high golden corn.

Such stories are a salutary reminder of the ultimate purpose of machine guns.

In a sense, developments in machine guns at both tactical and technical levels in the post-war period are far less dramatic than the developments pre-1945. (Submachine gun technology is a possible exception – see later chapter on this variant.) Rather than make a blow-by-blow historical overview of this period, therefore, it makes more sense to look at the overall themes of continuity and change.

The status of machine guns has been affected, at least in modern armies, by the rise of other weapons systems. Most importantly, from the end of World War II the world's infantry have progressively been armed with assault rifles, weapons firing rifle-calibre bullets but capable of delivering full-auto fire. Classic weapons of this type include the Soviet/Russian AK47 series, the US M16 weapons (in service from the 1960s) and the British SA80. In a sense, the assault rifle has somewhat stolen the LMG's thunder, as now every infantryman is capable of putting down quite heavy fire.

Yet even assault rifles have their limitations, particularly in terms of range and sustained fire, so the second half of the nineteenth century saw a new series of LMGs take to the market. Much of this development was also powered by major international ammunition standardisation programmes. For NATO countries, the 7.62 x 51mm NATO round became standard issue in 1954. This powerful rifle round was not suited to full-auto fire from a personal weapon (although many tried), so a new breed of machine guns was required to take it. A superb design came from Belgium in the 1950s, when Fabrique Nationale

produced the Mitrailleuse d'Appui Général ('General Purpose Machine Gun'; MAG), a gas-operated GPMG with all the combat versatility of the MG42. To date, more than 70 countries have equipped themselves with the FN MAG, and it is the standard issue GPMG of the British Army and other major forces.

US forces also adopted the FN MAG in the 1990s, with the designation M240, having had a troubled experience with another 7.62mm design, the M60. The M60 entered service as the US Army's standard MMG in the early 1960s, and was thrust into combat in the jungles and mountains of Vietnam. There it revealed a critical flaw. Bizarrely, the barrel, gas mechanism and bipod all came as a single unit, but the gun wasn't provided with a handle to grip when the barrel was being changed. The result was that the gun team, if they needed to change the barrel (often in the middle of a firefight), had to wrestle with a red-hot barrel system while also attempting to keep the rest of the gun out of the mud. A special asbestos glove for handling the barrel was often lost.

Combined with other flaws, the M60 was a less than satisfying gun to use, and its maladies informed the switch to the FN MAG later on. The M60 did not disappear entirely, however, and steady improvements have led to a much better gun, the M60E3, with a more user-friendly barrel change facility.

The Soviet Union was taking a different approach to machine gun development in the 1950s and 60s. The AK rifle fires a true assault cartridge, the 7.62 x 39mm M1943, being of full rifle calibre but with

◄◄ *The gas-operated FN MAG is one of history's most successful machine guns. Firing from a metal-link belt, it has commanding firepower at ranges well over a mile.*

Did you know?
The problems with the M60 machine gun led to its being given the nickname 'the Pig' by US soldiers during the Vietnam War.

➤ *French soldiers make a barrel change during training with the 7.5mm AAT-52. This belt-feed machine gun can take either light or heavy barrels, making it a true general-purpose machine gun.*

➤➤ *The Fabrique Nationale Minimi fires the 5.56mm round used in conventional NATO rifles. Here we can see the plastic ammunition box containing a 200-round belt.*

The AK series of assault rifles is the most mass-produced weapons system in history, with an estimated 80 million units manufactured since the late 1940s. Such ubiquity means machine guns like the RPK can take advantage of near universal ammunition supply.

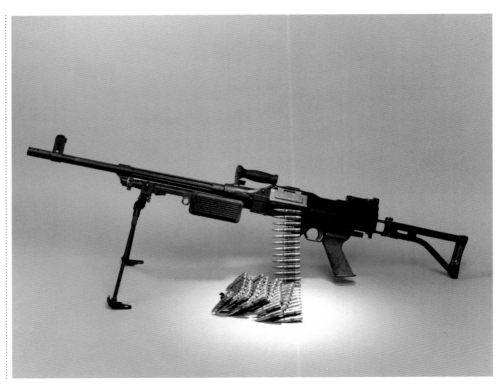

► The South African Vektor SS-77 is a 7.62mm NATO machine gun developed in the late 1970s and early 1980s. It is a gas-operated weapon firing at 600–900rpm.

The British Light Support Weapon (LSW) is little more than a heavy-barrelled version of the SA80 rifle. With a selective fire facility, it is also a decent sniper weapon.

◄ The Stoner modular weapons system was popular with Special Forces soldiers, such as this SEAL in Vietnam. His Stoner is fitted with a 100-round belt-feed drum magazine.

◄◄ The Browning M2HB soldiers on, here in its Quick-Change Barrel (QCB) modification, which as its name suggests allows for more rapid barrel changes.

➤ US Marines in Vietnam in 1966 fire 'the Pig', the 7.62mm M60 machine gun. Parts of the gun were based on the MG42, but the M60 failed to achieve the good reputation of the German weapon.

➤➤ An M134 Minigun stands in the doorway of a UH-1 helicopter in Vietnam. Miniguns were often used to spray down hostile landing zones as troops made airborne deployments.

a shortened case to produce less recoil, and to make the gun easier to control. The M1943 round became standardised throughout the Eastern Bloc, and the first machine gun to take the round was the RPD, a development of the wartime DP and DPM machine guns. Yet in the early 1960s, the RPD was replaced by the RPK, which is essentially just an AK rifle but fitted with a longer, heavier barrel, a bipod and a more durable stock. The design of the RPK not only meant that any infantryman would be able to operate it, but also that it accepted standard 30-round AK magazines as well as more capacious 40-round boxes or 75-round drums. The RPK admirably filled the LMG requirement, while the GPMG role was eventually taken by the PK family of machine guns, which has a quick-change barrel facility (the RPK's

Did you know?

The typical muzzle velocity of a 7.62 x 51mm NATO round is 2,690ft/sec (820m/sec), while the 5.56 x 45mm NATO round travels about 3,280ft/sec (1000m/sec). The larger, heavier round, however, tends to perform better over long ranges, and carries greater physical impact.

▶ The Soviet/Russian PKM LMG, here seen in the hands of Polish Army soldiers, fires the same 7.62mm round as the AK rifle. It weighs a mere 18.5lb (8.4kg).

▶▶ Polish troops demonstrate PKM and AK firepower during a night exercise. Rate of fire for the PKM is 710rpm.

A recent experimental multi-barrel machine gun system called 'Metal Storm', achieved cyclical rates of fire of one million rpm. It does so by firing the rounds, which are stacked up inside each barrel, electrically rather than using conventional mechanical mechanisms.

barrel is fixed), belt feed and fires the more powerful 7.62 x 54R cartridge.

Turning back to the West, change came in major style during the 1960s and 70s. In the 1960s, the US Army adopted the M16 as its standard infantry rifle. This rifle fired a 5.56 x 45mm round, a small but very high-velocity bullet that delivered much more controllable recoil in full-auto rifles. Once this step had been taken, the movement to standardise all NATO forces to this round was inexorable, and occurred in the following decade.

It made sense to design LMGs that were compatible with standard rifle ammunition, so 5.56mm LMGs soon emerged. An early, and extremely innovative design, was the Stoner 63 weapons system. Designed by one Eugene Stoner, the Stoner 63 was less an individual weapon than a modular firearm that could be configured into various different options. The receiver and gas mechanism were the fixed elements, but various barrels, feed systems and stocks could be fitted to make the gun into either an assault rifle, carbine, an LMG or MMG. The Stoner was ingenious, and did see combat use in Special Forces hands in Vietnam, but its complexity and operating flaws meant it was not a success, and few were made.

Far greater success in refining the 5.56mm machine gun came, once again, from FN in Belgium. Introduced in 1974, the Minimi is a light (15lb/6. 8kg) gas-operated machine gun with a handy feed mechanism that can accept a 200-round belt (fed from a box) or a standard M16 type 30-round box magazine. (The gun has two separate feed apertures, one for the belt, the other for the box.) Its rate of fire is between 700 and 1,150rpm, the rate varying according to which gas setting is used and whether box or belt feed is chosen (the box magazine produces faster firing, as the mechanism is free from pulling through the weight of the belt). Adopted by more than 30 countries worldwide (with various names), the Minimi occupies the summit of the LMG design. Note also that a 7.62mm version is also produced.

The Minimi is far from alone in its field, and almost all firearms-producing countries have produced LMGs of similar type. Germany has the HK13E, Britain has the Light Support Weapon (essentially nothing more than a long-barrelled SA80), Israel has the Negev (another gun with multiple feed options) and Italy the AR70-90. Spain revisited the MG42 by producing the belt-fed Cetme Ameli, largely an MG42 scaled down and recalibrated for 5.56mm ammunition. In short, the LMG type is as important as ever to today's armies.

SUBMACHINE GUNS

There is one side-development of the machine gun that so far we have not explored – the submachine gun (SMG). Strictly speaking, the SMG resides outside the pages of this book, as machine guns are classified as those weapons firing rifle-calibre cartridges in full-auto mode. The 'sub' part of the SMG titles refers to the fact that this class of weapon fires pistol-calibre cartridges.

They are only fed from magazines, never belts, and are free of bipods, tripods and other external mounts – they are purely hand-held weapons. Yet it would be remiss not to provide at least an overview of their development, such is their importance to the story of automatic fire.

SMGs emerged specifically out of the conditions of World War I. Rifles were good for long-range fire, but in trench combat soldiers soon discovered they needed heavy close-range firepower in a compact weapon that could be manoeuvred easily, not a weighty and lengthy rifle that needed recocking after every shot and had a range of more than a mile. The need was partly met by pistols and revolvers, but soon military engineers realized that the pistol-calibre cartridge could be allied to the auto mechanisms that were already developed.

The result was the SMG, and the forefather was the Italian Vilar-Perosa, introduced in 1915. This curious weapon featured two barrels and mechanisms linked together, firing 9mm pistol rounds at a rate of 1,200rpm from two 25-round detachable box magazines. It was blowback operated, as are almost all SMGs to date, the pistol cartridge not being powerful enough to require a locked breech. (Although many SMGs do have delaying mechanisms to allow pressures to drop to safe levels before the bolt opens.)

The Vilar-Perosa was not a commercial success, but it proved the concept of the SMG. This concept was then defined by the Germans with the Bergmann MP18, a 9mm blowback gun fed from a 32-shot helical drum magazine. The MP18 looked like a modern SMG, it was reliable and, at close

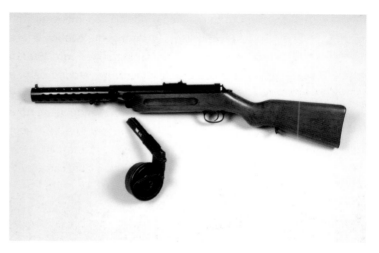

range, it was a fearsome gun that became known as the 'trench broom' on account of its 400rpm firepower.

The war ended with SMGs having received only a limited airing, but during the interwar period more nations brought

▲ *The Bergmann MP18 was the first operationally practical SMG, developed in 1916. Here we see the gun and its distinctive 32-round helical drum magazine.*

Selective fire means that the gun can be switched between single shots and full-auto fire. Some modern assault rifles and SMGs also have a two- or three-round burst facility, a fixed number of multiple shots being fired with a single trigger pull.

► *The MP40, the defining model of German SMG during World War II, utilised the 9mm Parabellum cartridge. The 'MP' suffix stood for 'Maschinenpistole' (Machine Pistol).*

out their own versions. The Finns produced the excellent 9mm Suomi Model 31, a high-quality SMG that fired at 900rpm and could take magazines varying from a 20-round box to a 71-round drum. The Czechs brought out the ZK 383, another 9mm gun that was so dependable that it could also double as an LMG when using its integral bipod. Great Britain made no serious investment in SMG technology before 1939, an oversight that it would struggle to fix when war broke out in that year. Germany, by contrast, kept up the momentum by producing the MP28II (a selective-fire version of the MP18), the progressive MP34/I and MP35/I, and, just before the war, the legendary MP38.

Unlike most other SMGs, the MP38 was made entirely of steel, a tubular design encasing a simple blowback mechanism. The 32-round box vertical magazine formed part of the front grip. The MP38 was a true combat weapon, but when war broke out, Germany, along with all the other combatants, discovered a significant problem with existing SMG designs. The

MP38 was good, but in a sense it was too good – it was made using machining processes that were too slow and expensive for wartime emergency conditions. Thus was born the MP40, which had the same layout and operating mechanism as the MP38, but was produced using lower-grade metals, pressings and stampings instead of machining, and spot-welded joints. In this format some one million MP40s were made during the war, giving the frontline German soldiers substantial close-range firepower.

Other nations quickly bought into the idea of cheap, mass-produced submachine guns. The weapons that consequently emerged where often astonishingly crude – such as the 9mm Sten Gun and the US M3 – but most importantly they could be churned out in great numbers. Some two million Sten Mk 2s, for example, were produced in only three years. The Soviets manufactured five million of their excellent, robust 7.62mm PPSh-41 machine guns, a

▼ The US M3 SMG was cheap and quick to make, and some 680,000 were produced between 1943 and 1945. It was known as the 'Grease Gun' by US troops.

Did you know?

The most famous US SMG of the post-World War I era was the Thompson, a .45-calibre weapon designed by John T. Thompson. It was heavily used by police and gangsters alike during the 1920s and 1930s, and in its M1/M1A1 versions equipped US soldiers during World War II and beyond.

weapon that kept on working regardless of the elements and that ran through a 35-round box magazine or 71-round drum magazine at 900rpm.

The SMG proved invaluable for urban warfare, but with the end of World War II in 1945 its future quickly looked precarious. The assault rifle, which could fire full-auto but had much better range and accuracy, suddenly appeared to make the SMG redundant. Yet in the post-war

◄ A British paratrooper holds the Sten Mk II, of which two million were produced during World War II. The numerous versions of the Sten included the Mk IIS suppressed version.

◄◄ British troops fire the M1928 Thompson SMG. Thompsons could be loaded with either 18-, 20- or 30-round box magazines, or 50- or 100-round drum magazines.

Despite its ungainly appearance, the Australian 9mm Owen SMG was both easy to handle and resilient. Its superb performance in jungle warfare led to its being kept in reserve stocks for decades after the war.

Did you know?

One reason why hostage-rescue forces prefer SMGs to rifles is that the pistol-calibre rounds have less of a risk of 'over-penetration' – going through the target and potentially striking hostages, civilians or comrades beyond. Expanding pistol rounds tend to stop within the body of the target

world the SMG has found two ready but contrasting markets – Special Forces and insurgents. Both markets demand compact short-range firepower, as they mainly fight within urban scenarios, typically on opposite sides of hostage-rescue missions.

One seminal development of the post-war SMG was essentially miniaturisation. The Czechs led the way with the CZ 23, 24, 25 and 26 guns during the late 1940s and early 1950s. Here were guns that had the magazine fitted directly into the pistol grip, and also featured a wrap-around bolt – the front of the bolt is tubular and actually wraps around the end of the barrel. The overall result was that the guns were very short, especially as the later

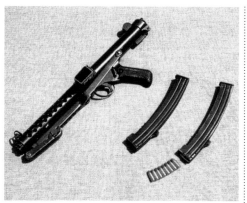

The Sterling was the British Army's standard SMG during the post-war period. Unusually, it had a side feed magazine and could also be fitted with a bayonet.

models had folding metal stocks – the stock-folded length of the CZ 24 was just 17.5in (445mm). The greatest of this type of SMG, however, was undoubtedly the Uzi. With a cyclical rate of 600rpm, since the 1950s the Uzi has offered portable firepower not only to Israel Defence Forces (IDF) soldiers, but also thousands of Special

◄◄ The Soviet PPSh-41 was a tough weapon with a 900rpm rate of fire. Here it is fitted with the 71-round drum magazine, but it also took 35-round box magazines.

Forces and law enforcement personnel in more than 30 countries, and large numbers of criminals. Miniaturisation could go to extreme levels – the Micro-Uzi variant is just 9.84in (250mm) with its stock folded and fires at 1,250rpm.

Such is not to say that SMGs with conventional layout have fallen by the wayside. The British Army, for example, between the 1950s and 1980s equipped many of its soldiers with the 9mm Sterling SMG, a gun visually recognised by its perforated barrel jacket and side-mounted magazine. The German Heckler & Koch MP5 series is used internationally to this day by specialist police and military units (it was famously seen in the hands of the SAS unit breaking the Iranian Embassy Siege in 1980), who appreciate its superb accuracy, even firing on full-auto. The series is extremely diverse, and ranges from the standard MP5, through to the MP5K shortened version and even a suppressed (the correct term for 'silenced') version, the MP5SD.

Such weapons have kept SMGs relevant to this day.

◄ *The 5.7mm FN P90 is classed as a Personal Defence Weapon. Intended as a back-up weapon for vehicle operators or rear-echelon troops, it is extremely compact but delivers high firepower. Note the plastic magazine running flat across the gun's receiver.*

A US Navy SEAL demonstrates the world's most successful post-war SMG, the Heckler & Koch MP5. Firing from a closed bolt (only the firing pin moves when the gun is first fired), the MP5 is both accurate and powerful.

Turning back to machine guns proper, we have already seen the continuing importance of LMGs. In terms of medium and heavy machine guns, most of these types remain in use fixed to vehicles or helicopters, the latter either as door-mounted guns or set in computer-aimed gun pods operated by the pilot or weapons operator. Few fixed-wing combat aircraft today include pure machine guns as part of their armament, although fighters and ground-attack planes typically retain a cannon – an automatic weapon much like a machine gun but firing large calibre (20mm+) explosive rounds. There is also another machine gun that takes us back almost full circle to where we started our journey. Developed for use aboard US helicopters in Vietnam, the 7.62mm GE Minigun M134 bears a distinct resemblance to the Gatling gun, being a six-barrel rotary weapon. The key difference with the Gatling, however, is that the Minigun is driven by an electric motor to achieve rates of fire up to 6,000rpm. Since it emerged during the 1960s, the Minigun and its derivatives have gone on to be a heavy-firepower fitting to numerous aircraft and also combat vehicles and naval vessels, from Cobra attack helicopters to US destroyers. The Minigun illustrates as much as any modern machine gun, that while machine gun technology has undoubtedly progressed, the fundamental designs established in the late nineteenth and first half of the twentieth century still hold currency. Indeed, looking at machine guns in general, it is impressive that weapons whose operating systems have more than 100 years of ancestry behind them are still as relevant on the battlefield today as they always were.

GLOSSARY

Action: The operating parts of the gun responsible for cartridge feed, cartridge ejection and firing.

Assault rifle: A magazine-fed automatic rifle firing a cartridge of power between that of a pistol and a rifle.

BAR: Browning Automatic Rifle

Blowback-operated: A system of firearms operation in which the bolt is not locked on firing; when the gun is fired, breech pressure against the cartridge forces the bolt backwards to cycle the gun.

Bolt: The part of a gun, often including the firing pin, that closes the breech before firing. The bolt is often used to perform cartridge loading and extraction.

Breech: The rear aperture of the gun barrel, where the cartridge is loaded for firing.

Breech block: The part of the gun responsible for sealing the breech of the gun for firing. Although the term can also mean the same as 'bolt' (*q.v.*), 'breech block' tends to apply to large rectangular mechanisms, whereas bolt applies to cylindrical rotating mechanisms.

Cartridge: A unit of ammunition, composed of the bullet, case (containing the propellant) and the primer.

Chamber: The section at the rear of a gun barrel in which the cartridge is seated prior to firing.

Ejection: Refers to the system by which a spent cartridge is thrown clear of the gun.

Extraction: Refers to the system by which a spent cartridge is removed from the chamber ready for ejection.

Gas-operated: A system of firearms operation that uses gas pressure to perform the cycle of loading and extraction.

GPMG:	General Purpose Machine Gun
HMG:	Heavy Machine Gun
LMG:	Light Machine Gun
Magazine:	A box or drum casing, often detachable, used to hold ammunition and feed it into a gun mechanism.
MMG:	Medium Machine Gun
Muzzle:	The front end of a gun barrel.
Muzzle velocity:	The velocity of the bullet as it leaves the muzzle of the gun.
Primer:	A cap in the base of a cartridge containing an impact-detonated explosive compound. This compound is detonated by the firing pin, and thereby detonates the main cartridge charge.
Recoil-operated:	A system of cycling a gun by using the recoil forces generated on firing. Short recoil means the barrel and bolt unlock after a very short distance of travel backwards, while in long recoil they unlock once they have covered more than the distance of the unfired cartridge.
Rpm:	Rounds per minute
SMG:	Submachine gun

BIBLIOGRAPHY

Allsop, D.F. and M.A. Tooney, *Small Arms* (Brassey's, 1999)

Ellis, John, *The Social History of the Machine Gun* (Johns Hopkins University Press, 1989)

Ford, Roger, *The World's Great Machine Guns – From 1860 to the Present Day* (Brown Packaging, 1999)

Hogg, Ian V., *The Story of the Gun – From Matchlock to M16* (Boxtree, 1996)

Hogg, Ian V. and John Weeks, *Military Small Arms of the 20th Century* (Arms & Armour, 1991)

McNab, Chris, *Firearms – The Illustrated Guide to Small Arms of the World* (Paragon, 2008)

Pope, Dudley, *Guns* (London, Hamlyn Publishing, 1969)

Walter, John, *The Greenhill Dictionary of Guns and Gunmakers* (Greenhill, 2001)

Willbanks, James H., *Machine Guns: An Illustrated History of Their Impact* (ABC-CLIO, 2004)